The Beginner Book

Warfare by Duct Tape

DISCLAIMER AND TERMS OF USE AGREEMENT

ISBN-13:978-1-942006-01-5

Table of Contents

"Had I sons I should train them as your husband intends to train your son. It may be that he will never be called upon to draw a sword, but the time he has spent in acquiring its use will not be wasted. These exercises give firmness and suppleness to the figure, quickness to the eye, and briskness of decision to the mind. A man who knows that he can at need defend his life if attacked, whether against soldiers in the field or robbers in the street, has a sense of power and self-reliance that a man untrained in the use of the strength God has given him can never feel. I was instructed in arms when a boy, and I am none the worse for it."   - G. A. Henty

St. Bartholomew's Eve

Description of the Battle Game

Battling is at least two teams fighting each other using weapons. We suggest using our foam weapons to minimize injuries.

Divide your players into two teams of about the same strength and even numbers. Say there are four big guys and four little guys. There should be two big guys and two little guys on each team.

Weather is no deterrent to battling. We have had battles in rain and heat.

Object of the game: divide and conquer your enemy!

More than one battle can be played. It is important to keep score of who wins each battle. The one who wins the most battles is the victor!

You can use fortifications. Tree houses work well. Piles of logs or even swing sets can be used.

Naval battles can be fought using non-motor boats such as canoes and row boats. To fight a naval battle, simply row up to them and fight them. Do not use throwing axes, they are not waterproof.

With fortifications, it is often wise to use your spear instead of your axe or sword. The spear has greater length which is helpful in forts. It is very wise to use missiles (water balloons, throwing axes, etc.) so you can bombard the enemy without having to storm the gate.

It is crucial to use shields. People who do not use shields are usually slain early in the battle and are vulnerable to throwing axes and heavy weapons such as battle axes.

Terrible war cries intimidate the enemy.

It is important to have one main leader (general). This keeps the army unified and reduces squabbles.

Rules of the Battle Game

Rule #1
Chivalry and honor must be exhibited at all times.

Rule #2
If any weapon hits your limb (for ex. arm, leg, hand), you are no longer able to use it.

If you are holding a weapon in the hand or arm that is hit, you can't keep using the weapon with that arm but could switch it to the other arm and keep fighting. If both arms are hit, you must surrender or run away.

If your leg is hit, you must limp. If both legs are hit, you must kneel or squat. If you lose all your limbs, you are doomed!

Rule #3
If you get hit in the head, neck or torso, you are officially dead and can't play until the end of the battle.

Rule #4
The only way to win a battle is when all of the enemy (other team) are dead, have surrendered or have run away (escaped).

If a team holding prisoners is defeated, the prisoners are automatically freed.

Rule #5
If someone surrenders, you can either keep them captive, (they are not allowed to escape) or release them and they are free to return to their army (team).

Rule #6
Parley~ a parley is when one or possibly two people from each team talk to each other. To start a parley, one team member must say, "Request an audience". If the other team agrees, they send a person forward to talk to the other.

It is usually used for discussing the release of prisoners by ransom or switching of players. You can be chivalrous and release prisoners. It is important to not carry weapons but must leave them behind during a parley to avoid treachery.

Rule #7
We believe that only boys should battle with other boys. Young men should practice protecting young ladies so it is not appropriate to fight them.

Rule #8
Ransom~A ransom is when a soldier who is captured is released by a payment of money. You can make your own money (see instructions). To ransom a prisoner, first call a parley and then negotiate the price. A general usually costs more than the average soldier. (This rule is optional.)

Weapon Instructions

Introduction:

PVC pipe tips: You can find PVC pipe at your local hardware store like Lowe's and Home Depot. You will need a saw to cut the PVC pipe to the correct length. If you do not have a saw, the large hardware stores will usually cut it for you.

PVC pipe insulation~the black foam stuff. We usually buy this at the same stores as the PVC pipe. We like the kind that comes in a 4 pack of 3 foot pieces.

Foam~the 2 inch thick green stuff. You can find this foam at Wal-Mart and fabric stores like JoAnn's and Hobby Lobby. It comes in small packages or in large pieces by the yard.

Cardboard: It can be difficult to cut cardboard so younger kids might need some help or supervision. In most of the pieces that use cardboard, it is important to cut the cardboard so the "ridges" (inner corrugated sections) **run across** the narrow width of the piece. This way the piece can bend properly. Check instructions before tracing the pattern onto the cardboard.

½ Width Piece of Duct Tape: Before we begin the weapon instructions, we need to define a term we will use in the book: "½ width". To make a ½ width piece of duct tape, take a piece of duct tape and tear it lengthwise (the long way). Now you have two ½ width pieces of duct tape. Sometimes, even a ¼ width piece of duct tape is used. Just tear the ½ width piece again to make the ¼ width.

Now, on to the fun!

Short Sword

Materials:

2 foot piece of ¾ inch PVC pipe
2 foot piece of PVC pipe insulation
(We use 3/8" thick polyethylene foam, fits ¾" pipe)
Duct tape
Scissors
(You may need a saw to cut the PVC to size)
Please Note: This project may require adult help to use the sharp tools.

Directions:

Cut 5 inches off of your 2 foot piece of insulation.

Next, take the larger piece of insulation and slide it down the 2-foot PVC pipe.

Leave about 1 inch extending off of the PVC at the point of the sword.

Take the 5 inch piece of insulation foam. Cut a slit 2 inches long in the center and again on the back so they line up. Don't cut on the seam. It will weaken it.

Slide the piece of foam onto the PVC pipe to form the hilt of the sword.

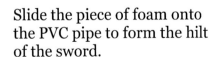

Crisscross the duct tape around the hilt to strengthen it.

Tape across the end of the hilt, turn and do it again. Then tape around the end to make it smooth.

Do this on both ends of the hilt. Cover the entire hilt with duct tape.

Be sure to wrap around the pipe/ handle.

Tape the point (end) of the sword blade the same way. Wrap the duct tape around a few times to strengthen it so it won't tear during battle.

Now tape the blade. It is helpful to have another person. Start at the hilt and wrap on a slightly diagonal angle towards the tip of the blade.

Cover the handle. Cap the end just as you did with the end of the blade.

Decorate as desired. You are done!!

Dagger

Materials:

6 inch piece of ¾ inch PVC pipe
8 inch piece of PVC pipe insulation
(We use 3/8" thick polyethylene foam, fits ¾" pipe)
Duct tape
Scissors/ Ruler
Saw (You may need a saw to cut the PVC to size)

Please Note: This project may require adult help to use the sharp tools.

Directions:

Slide the insulation onto the PVC pipe leaving 4 inches for the handle.

Tape across the end of the insulation at the tip of the spear, turn and repeat. Then tape around the end to make it smooth.

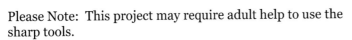

Starting at the tip, wrap the duct tape on a slightly diagonal angle until the insulation is covered and just onto the PVC pipe.

Using a ½ width piece of duct tape, tape around the base of the blade over

the PVC pipe to reinforce it.

Cover handle with the color of your choice, tucking in the ends as you go. Decorate as desired.

Throwing Axe

Materials:

1 piece of foam 5 ½" by 11" by 2" thick
Duct tape
Scissors
Marker
Pattern

Directions:

Print and cut out the pattern. Lay the pattern on the foam, trace the throwing axe on the foam using a permanent marker and then cut it out.

Cover the handle with duct tape the color of your choice. Carefully tape the end so that the corners stay square.

It is important to put a piece of duct tape on the side of the axe as shown in the picture to reinforce the axe. This prevents the throwing axe from tearing when you throw it. Do this on both sides.

Press duct tape firmly to foam.

Pinch the edges so they don't get dirty.

Cover the inside of the blade.

 Starting on the sides, cover the blade, being careful to keep the edges square.

Using the same technique, you can make throwing knives.

Make up your own shapes and designs.

DO NOT USE IN WATER!! They might get moldy. They are not waterproof.

Club

Materials:

16 inch piece of ¾ inch PVC pipe
14 inch piece of PVC pipe insulation
(We use 3/8" thick polyethylene foam, fits ¾" pipe)
Foam 2' thick, scraps, or about 12" x 12"
Duct tape
Scissors
Ruler
(You may need a saw to cut the PVC to size)
    Please Note: This project may require adult help to use the sharp tools.
You may make this club larger or smaller. Just make as you like.

Directions:

Cut a 1 ½ inch piece of pipe insulation (black) and put it on one end of the PVC pipe.

Take the rest of the pipe insulation (black) and slide it onto the other end. Leave a space that is comfortable for your hand. That space is the handle of the club.

Cut off the excess black insulation at the end of the PVC pipe.

Now to make the head of the club: This weapon is excellent for using scraps of green foam. The measurements are not exact, use a scrap piece that is about the same size if you like.

Take a piece of (green) foam about 5 inches by 3 ½ inches. Put it on the side. Take a big piece of duct tape and wrap the foam onto the club handle. Be sure that it is **not** too tight. Make sure the tape goes all the way around the handle.

Do this 3 times around the end of the club. Be sure the tape is not too tight.

Tape over the foam forming it into a ball shape as you go. Secure it to the handle.

You may have places that need a little more foam to make it round. Just add a small piece of foam and tape over it.

 Tape around the handle at the base of the ball to secure the duct tape.

Add a top piece of foam about 4" x 4 1/2" or whatever looks good to you. Tape it down in a crisscross then cover the rest of the foam with duct tape.

Now for the handle:
Wrap a piece of duct tape so it is half way onto the black insulation at the handle. Press the duct tape down. Wrap a piece of duct tape around that area. We used a ½ width of tape. (Just tear a piece of duct tape in half long way.)

Put a short piece of duct tape over the end of the handle and press in the edges for a smooth look. Turn and repeat.

Wrap a piece of duct tape around the base. Press the edge and wrap a half width piece of duct tape around it.

Decorate to your liking!

The Spikes...these are optional but here you go.

Cut 4 squares of foam. (Or as many as you need for the number of spikes that you want.)

These squares were 2 1/2" x 2". But the size can vary depending on the size of your club. You can make them bigger or smaller.

Trim the edges of the squares. Cut about half way down the edge. Do this on all 4 edges.

Then trim again to make a point. Keep trimming until you get a nice looking spike.

Place a piece of tape on one side of the spike and make sure the ends of the tape hang off so it can attach to the ball. Then place the spike on the club when you want it to go. Press down the edges of the tape. Add another piece of tape around the other side of the spike and press it down.

Get some smaller pieces of duct tape and finish covering the spike. Try to not use too much tape or it will make it too hard and heavy.

Repeat this for all of the spikes. You can place them wherever you like.

You are done! Great job!!

Cardboard Shield

Materials:

Cardboard~whatever size you desire, we used 2 pieces of 16" x 15", plus 13" x 6"
Duct Tape
Scissors
Ruler

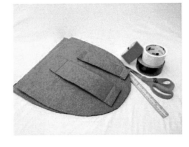

Directions:

First, you must decide what shape you want for the shield. We used a middle era Knight shield. But you can choose whatever shape you like.

Cut the cardboard to the shape that you choose. You need two (2) of them. The best way to cut the pieces is so that the grain of the cardboard is going in different directions. One piece could go up and down and the other piece has grain that goes across the shield. This keeps it from bending.

Tape the 2 pieces together spacing the duct tape around the edge of the shield. This is for strength.

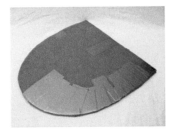 

Completely cover the edge, taping from the front to the back, all the way around of the shield.

Cover the back of the shield with duct tape.

Decorate the front as desired.

To make the straps:

(You may need to modify this to fit the style of shield that you have chosen.)

Please note: For the cardboard arm band pieces, be sure to cut the cardboard so the "ridges" (inner corrugated sections) **run across** the narrow width of the piece. This way the piece can bend properly.

Cut a piece of cardboard 13 inches long by 2 inches wide. Cut another piece of cardboard 13 inches long by 3 inches wide. (Or smaller if you have a smaller shield.)

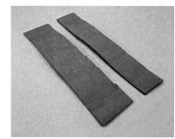

Leave one inch flat on each end and then crease the pieces so they have a nice curve.

Cover the cardboard strips with duct tape.

Place the strips on the back of the shield where you want them. The wider 3 inch strip should go near the forearm. The narrow strip is for the hand grip. Use a small piece of tape to hold the strips in place while you try it out. Be sure to give your arm plenty of room. Adjust the strips if needed.

   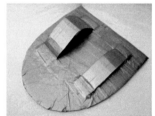

Tape over the ends.   Reinforce the ends by cross taping the duct tape again. Use plenty of tape so the arm bands are secure.

You're done!

Buckler

Materials:

Duct tape
Lid from a wheat bucket or ice cream tub
    or a piece of plywood cut into a circle 13" in diameter or size of your choice

Directions:

Cover the lid with tape. Start with strips across the middle. Cover the entire front.

To make the straps on the back, lay a piece of duct tape sticky side up.

Then cover with a longer strip that goes over the edges. Put 3 more strips over the top of the strap to strengthen it.

Cover the edge with duct tape and decorate as desired. This is the time to let your artistic talent shine!

Helmet

Materials:

Patterns
Cardstock
Cardboard~at least 13" x 9"
Duct Tape
Scissors
Clear "scotch" tape
Elastic~about ¾" wide by about 8 or 9 inches long
Stapler/Staples
Ruler

> Please Note: This project may require adult help to use the sharp tools.

Directions:

Print the helmet pieces on **cardstock** and cut them out.

You will need the helmet pieces: Upper helmet piece, Lower helmet piece, Helmet nose guard, and Back of Helmet. (If you want the helmet in a smaller size, try minimizing the patterns on a copy machine.)

Please note: For all cardboard pieces, be sure to cut the cardboard so the "ridges" (inner corrugated sections) **run across** the narrow width of the piece. This way the piece can bend properly.

 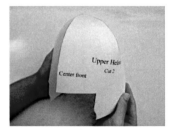

Tape together the upper helmet pieces at the center front with the "scotch" tape. Tape together the side edges at the top of the helmet pieces.

Cover the helmet neatly with duct tape, starting at the top. When you get to the dotted line, stop so you can add the lower piece here.

Trace the Lower helmet piece onto cardboard and cut out.

Also trace the Helmet nose guard piece onto cardboard and cut out.

Cover the Lower helmet piece on **both sides** with duct tape. Line up the Lower helmet piece at the dotted line on the Upper helmet piece and tape it firmly, inside and outside.

Cover the Helmet nose guard piece with duct tape on **both sides**. Try on the helmet and adjust the nose guard to cover your nose. Tape it firmly to the helmet, inside and outside.

Finish covering the helmet with duct tape. Be sure to cover the inside of the helmet, too.

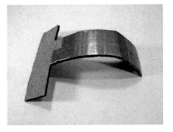

Trace the back of the helmet piece onto cardboard and cut out.

Be sure to cut the cardboard so the "ridges" (inner corrugated sections) **run across** the helmet piece. This way the piece can bend properly.

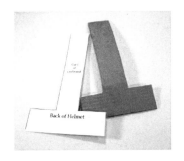 

Bend the long upper section of the back helmet piece into a curve to form around the head.

Cover upper section with duct tape inside and out.

Also bend the lower side sections into a curve and cover with duct tape inside and out.

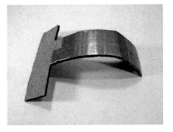 

Cut elastic into two (2) 4 ½ inch pieces. Staple the elastic to the inside of the helmet back piece at the bottom edges. **Please note:** Staple away from the inside so the point of the staples are not near the skin.

Cover the staples with duct tape.

Attach the back helmet piece to the top (crown) of the helmet with duct tape inside and outside. Secure with staples and then cover them with duct tape. (On both sides.) . **Please note:** Staple away from the inside so the point of the staples are not near the skin.

Tape the other loose end of elastic to the upper helmet piece. Try on the helmet and adjust fit if necessary. Attach elastic to upper helmet by stapling and then covering with duct tape. **Please note:** Staple away from the inside so the point of the staples are not near the skin.

You are done! Decorate to your liking!

Tunic

Materials:
Some sort of fabric-knit, sheets, curtains, or whatever you have
Belt or material for a sash
Scissors
Sewing machine or needle and thread

Directions:

First determine the size you will need. Some tunics went down to the knees and had no sleeves. They draped over the shoulders a little bit. The size of your fabric may determine the width or measure across the shoulders. Make it wide enough so that you can slip it over your head and shoulders and get the arms out of the arm holes. If you have enough fabric, double the length so you won't need to sew a seam across the shoulders.

Cut a hole for the head to go through. The No-Sew Option is to just pull the tunic over the head and use a belt to keep it around the waist.

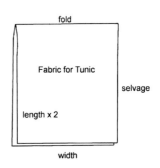

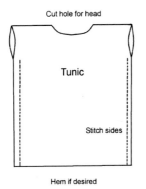

The sewing option is to sew up the sides but leave an arm hole. Hem the bottom if desired. Knit fabric is nice because it doesn't fray and you won't have to hem the edges.

If you want sleeves in your tunic, make a "T" shape of fabric and then sew up the sides. Be sure the main body of the tunic is wide enough so that you can get it on and get the arms through the sleeves. Maybe almost double the width across the front of the person.

Some children are small and the hole in the neck will gap too much. Just add a button and loop at the back of the neck to close it a little. See Cloak instructions.

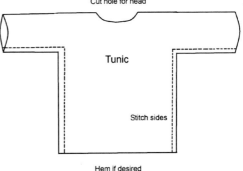

Use a belt or cut a strip of fabric to wrap around the waist.

Cloak

Materials:

Some sort of fabric-knit, sheets, curtains, or whatever you have
Button
Thin piece of elastic, ribbon, or string
Couple of pins
Scissors
Needle and thread

Directions:

Determine the size of cape that you need. Do you want a cloak that goes down to the knees or almost to the floor? That is your length measurement plus an inch to turn over at the neck. The width of your fabric may determine your width of the cloak, otherwise decide how wide you want it.

Cut your fabric to size. If you are using a fabric that will fray, you may want to hem the sides first. Fold over an inch the top edge which will go by the neck. Try it on. Clasp the cape closed a few inches down from the front of the neck. This where you will attach the button and elastic (ribbon). Mark it on both sides with a pin. Sew on the button on one side. Measure a small piece of elastic (ribbon) around the button so you can still get it on and off. Stitch elastic (ribbon) on both ends to the cape at the mark.

Throw over the shoulders and button at the neck.

Money Pouch

Materials:

Fabric: see instructions
String, rope, ribbon, shoe lace or whatever you have
Safety pin
Scissors
Sewing machine or needle and thread
Option: Leg from a pair of cut off pants

Directions:

You can make a money pouch out of almost anything. If you want a money pouch that is a bit fancier, you can use fabric. We just happened to have a scrap of velour that we used for a pouch. Knit fabric won't fray and is easier but any durable fabric will work.

Determine the size of pouch that you want. For example, if you want a pouch that is 5" x 7", allowing for seam allowances and the casing for the drawstring, cut two (2) squares of 6" x 8 ½". You can also cut a long rectangle and just fold over so that you eliminate one seam. The rectangle would be 6" x 16".

Put the right sides together and sew up the seams leaving one 6" side open (use ½" seam). Turn over 1" at the opening. Stitch around using a small seam of about ¼". On the side or center front, make a small cut in the casing only on the front piece big enough for the drawstring to go through.

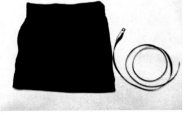

Cut your drawstring to at least twice the length of your opening. In this example, the opening is 10" after sewing, so the drawstring should be 20" long. Put the safety pin in the end of the drawstring and push it through the casing.

A leg from a pair of pants that was cut off into shorts can be made into a pouch. Cut to the size you want. Sew one end. Cut small slits about an inch apart and weave your drawstring in and out through the slits. If you don't have any, thrift stores and yard sales often have pants for cheap.

Coin Money for Ransom

Materials:

Aluminum foil
Something heavy like a hammer or shoe

Directions:

Take a small piece of aluminum foil about twice the size you want the coin to be and fold in the edges to make a circle. It's all right if it is not perfectly round, ancient money wasn't perfect either. Press down firmly against a hard surface and then hammer flat with the heel of a shoe or a hammer.

Mark the coins with designs or figures so you know which coins belong to you. You can also make a money pouch to keep your money in while you are battling. See instructions for money pouch.

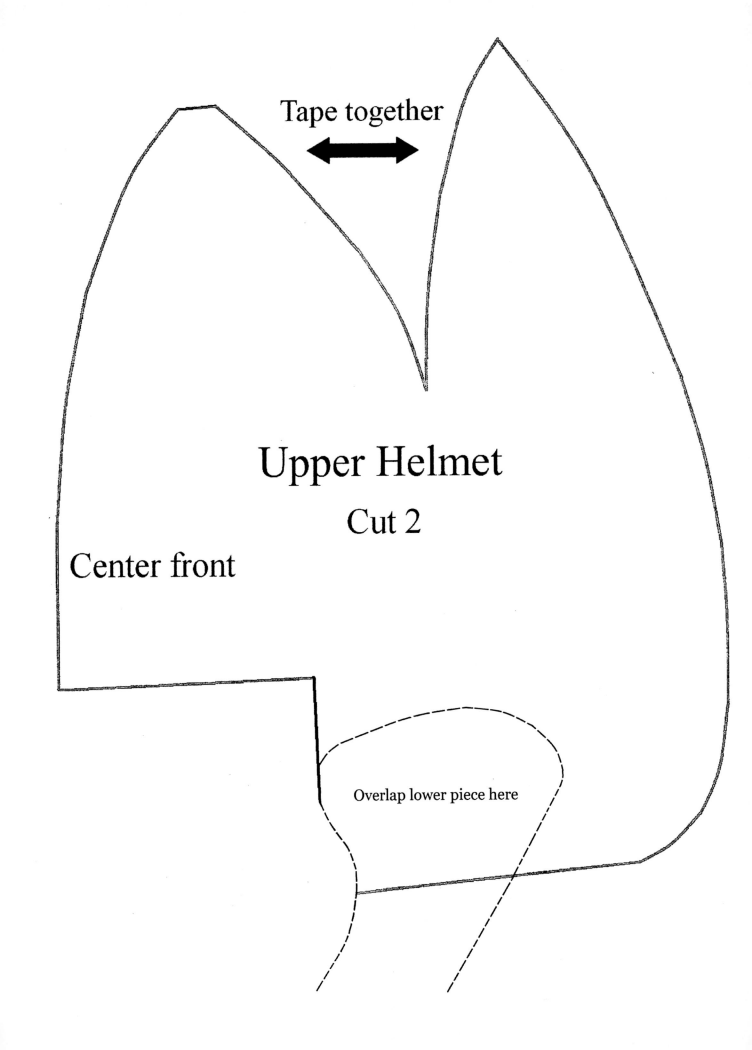

Tape together

Upper Helmet

Cut 2

Center front

Overlap lower piece here

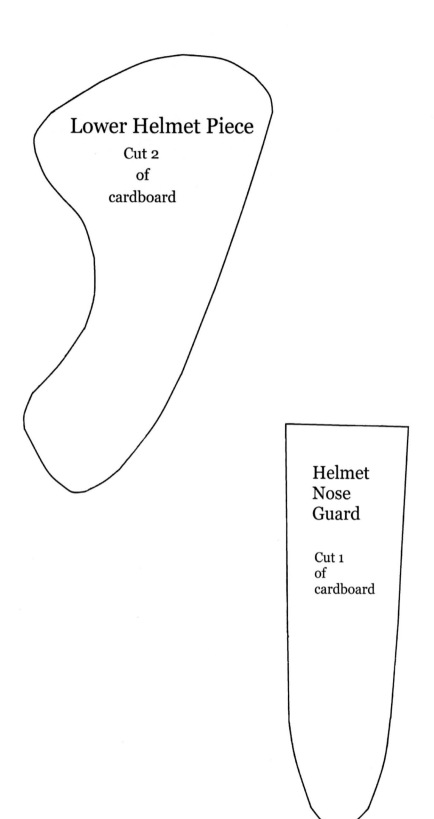

Lower Helmet Piece

Cut 2
of
cardboard

**Helmet
Nose
Guard**

Cut 1
of
cardboard

Cut 1
of
cardboard

Back of Helmet

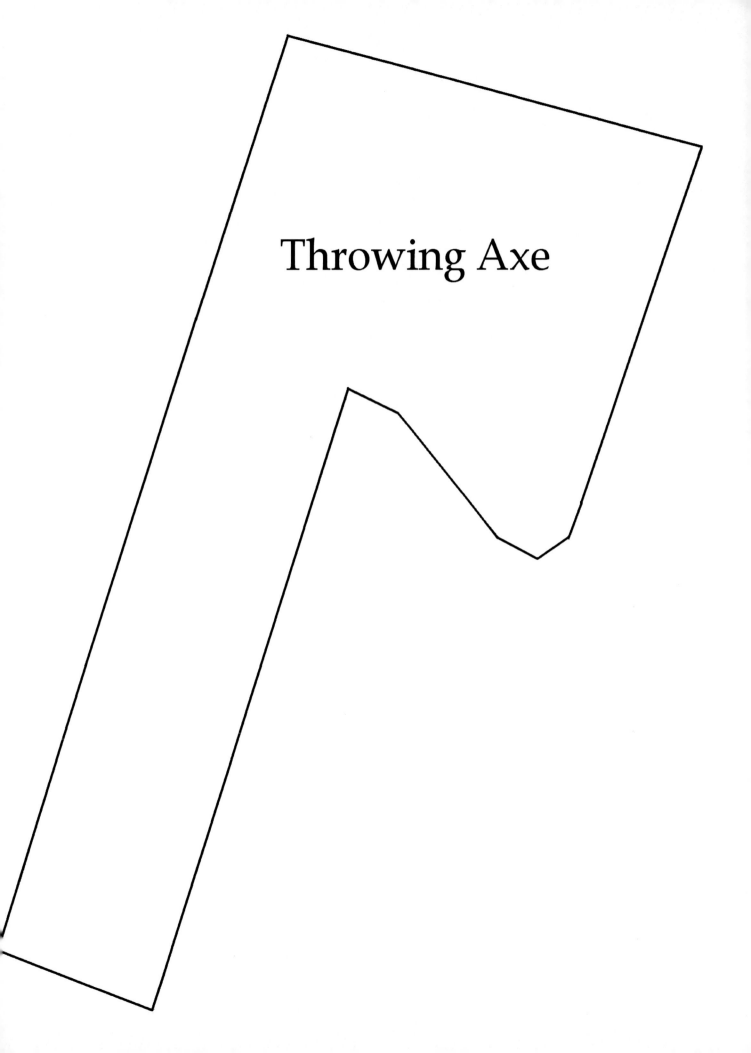

Throwing Axe

Visit our website **www.warfarebyducttape.com** for more information. Also available from Warfare by Duct Tape

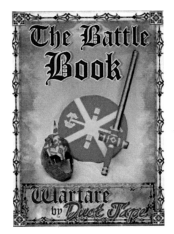  

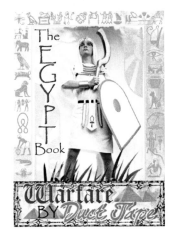